# This book belongs to:

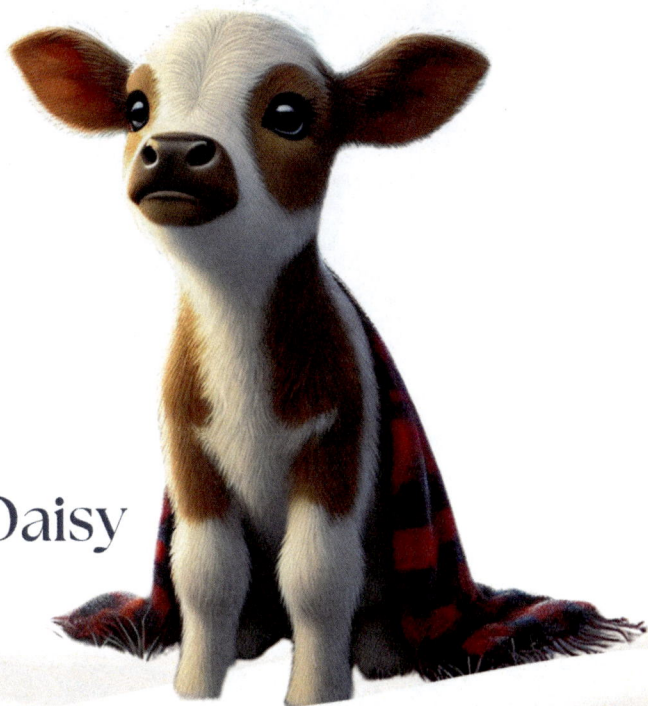

Meet Daisy

For my Father,
Who taught me the meaning of strength, fearlessness, and unwavering determination. Your faith in me, even in life's most challenging moments, has been my guiding light. This story is a testament to the values you instilled in me: To dream big, stay the course, and never give up.

With all my love and gratitude,
Dennita

**Daisy's Day on Santa's Sleigh**

For permission requests or inquiries, please contact the author directly.
Dennita Miskimen
dennita@redschoolhousenetwork.com


Published in United States of America.

ISBN: 9798300024697

Illustrations created with AI tools under the direction of the author.
First Edition.

In the quiet countryside of Virginia, on The Red Barn Farm, lived a little Zebu cow named Daisy.

Daisy was not only small—she was the tiniest Zebu on the farm, with a heart so big it practically shone.

Every night, while the world drifted off to sleep, Daisy would gaze up at the stars and whisper her one, true wish: to help Santa bring Christmas magic to the world.

One crisp December morning, Daisy gathered her courage and told the other barn animals about her wish. She spoke with so much hope that even the air around her seemed to listen.

But the big brown horse shook his head. "Daisy, only reindeer can lead Santa's sleigh." The wise old hen gave her a gentle smile, "You're so small, dear. Maybe you should dream a little smaller."

And even the kind, older cows nudged her softly, suggesting that she might be better off staying close to home, where it was safe.

Daisy's heart trembled a bit at their words, but then she remembered the feeling she had each night as she looked at the stars—the feeling that she was meant for something wonderful, something just big enough for her.

And so, she decided that no one could tell her how big her heart was, or how big her dreams should be.

Each day after that, Daisy trained by herself. She found an old, battered sled in the corner of the barn, and every morning, she would harness herself to it and pull it across the snowy fields, huffing and puffing with all her might.

She tied tiny bells around her neck, making her own jingle as she walked, and even crafted antlers from branches to wear as she practiced. Her small legs trembled from the effort, but her heart grew stronger with each step.

Every night, she would whisper her wish to the stars, and every night, she could almost feel them twinkling back at her, as if they, too, believed in her dream.

Finally, Christmas Eve arrived, and the air was filled with the magic and excitement of the season. Daisy watched as Santa's reindeer gathered, each one noble and proud, ready to set off on their journey.

But just then, Rudolph, the lead reindeer, appeared with a very red nose—not glowing, but sniffling. He looked tired and weak, unable to fly.

The barn animals murmured and gasped—Rudolph had come down with reindeer flu! He wouldn't be able to guide the sleigh tonight, and they all wondered how Santa would make it through the stormy winter sky without his lead.

Just then, Santa himself entered the barn, his face filled with worry. "I need a helper tonight," he said softly, scanning the barn. "Without someone brave to guide us, we may have to cancel Christmas."

The words echoed in the quiet barn, filling Daisy's heart with a sudden, fierce hope. This was her moment.

With a trembling breath, Daisy stepped forward, her bells jingling. The other animals looked on in surprise. "Daisy?" the horse asked softly. "You're so small, and it's a big job."

But Daisy only held her head high, looking at Santa with steady eyes. "I may be small," she said, her voice steady, "but I've trained for this, and I believe I can help."

Santa's eyes softened as he looked at Daisy, recognizing her courage and the warmth in her heart. He knelt down and whispered, "Christmas magic isn't just for the big and strong. It's for those with heart—and I believe you have enough heart for the whole world, Daisy."

With a twinkle in his eye, Santa sprinkled her with North Pole magic, and Daisy felt a gentle warmth spread through her.

Suddenly, her small hooves felt light as snowflakes, and her heart swelled with joy and love.

As the sleigh rose into the starry sky, Daisy took a deep, trembling breath, feeling the world open wide before her. She couldn't believe it—she, a little Zebu from The Red Barn Farm, was leading Santa's sleigh.

The stars above felt closer than they ever had, like old friends cheering her on, twinkling brightly as if to say, "We knew you could do it, Daisy."

With each farmhouse and village they passed, Daisy felt her heart grow warmer.

She saw soft lights glowing from windows, tiny wreaths on doors, and imagined children tucked in bed, dreaming of Christmas morning.

Daisy's heart swelled with love for each sleeping family below, and she wanted to give them every bit of joy and magic she had inside her.

The wind was strong, and the sleigh was heavy, but with every pull of her hooves, Daisy whispered to herself, I can do this. I was meant to do this.

She thought of her friends in the barn, her nightly wishes, and all the times she had trained alone in the snow. Every moment, every dream, had brought her to this.

As they flew over snowy fields and frosty trees, Daisy hummed Christmas carols softly to herself, her voice lifting into the quiet night. Her heart was so full it ached, not from sadness, but from something sweeter, something like love and hope and magic all at once.

Daisy looked back at Santa, who gave her a proud, gentle nod. She realized that it wasn't just her dream anymore— it was a gift she was sharing with the whole world, a gift that could only come from her heart.

By the time they reached the last farmhouse, Daisy felt as if she'd left pieces of her heart in every place they had flown, and in return, she carried with her the love and dreams of everyone below.

And in that moment, as the first light of dawn touched the horizon, Daisy understood that her dream had come true in ways she'd never imagined.

RED BARN

As dawn painted the snowy fields in hues of pink and gold, Santa and Daisy landed softly at The Red Barn Farm.

The barn doors slowly creaked open, and one by one, the animals emerged, their eyes wide with awe as they took in the sight before them.

The big brown horse stepped forward, his proud gaze softened with wonder. He lowered his head in a humble bow and said, "Daisy, you've done what we could only dream of."

The hen fluttered her wings, her eyes shining as she clucked, "You made the magic real, Daisy.

You brought Christmas to us all!" Even the wise old cows looked at her with tear-filled eyes, each of them murmuring, "We never imagined…" Their voices trailed off, overcome with a deep respect for the tiniest Zebu with the mightiest heart.

Santa knelt down beside Daisy, placing a gentle hand on her shoulder. "Daisy," he said, his voice warm and full of pride, "you've given a gift beyond all others. You've reminded us that sometimes, the smallest hearts carry the greatest magic.  You brought Christmas to life—not only for the children, but for all of us here tonight."

That morning, as Daisy nestled into her cozy corner of the barn, she felt a joy that was boundless—a joy that came from knowing she had touched the hearts of others. The warmth she felt wasn't just from the North Pole magic; it was the glow of self-belief and the love of her friends.

From that day forward, The Red Barn Farm became a place where dreams were nurtured and hearts were encouraged to soar. Daisy's journey was told and retold, inspiring every creature who heard it to believe in the power of their own dreams.

As Daisy gazed up at the fading stars, she no longer whispered wishes but words of gratitude.

She had learned that the true magic wasn't in the stars above but within her all along. And as she closed her eyes, she knew that no dream was too big, no dreamer too small, and that with heart and hope, anything was possible.

The End

Made in the USA
Las Vegas, NV
01 December 2024

13086277R10021